# Snowball Fight

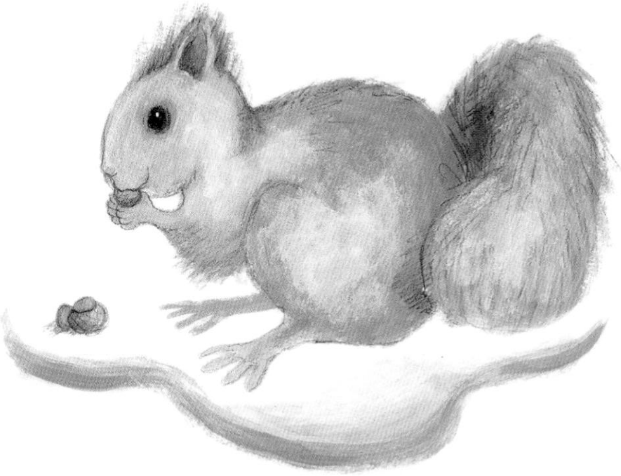

Paul Shipton
Illustrated by Lindsey Gardiner

Rigby
A Harcourt Achieve Imprint
www.Rigby.com
1-800-531-5015

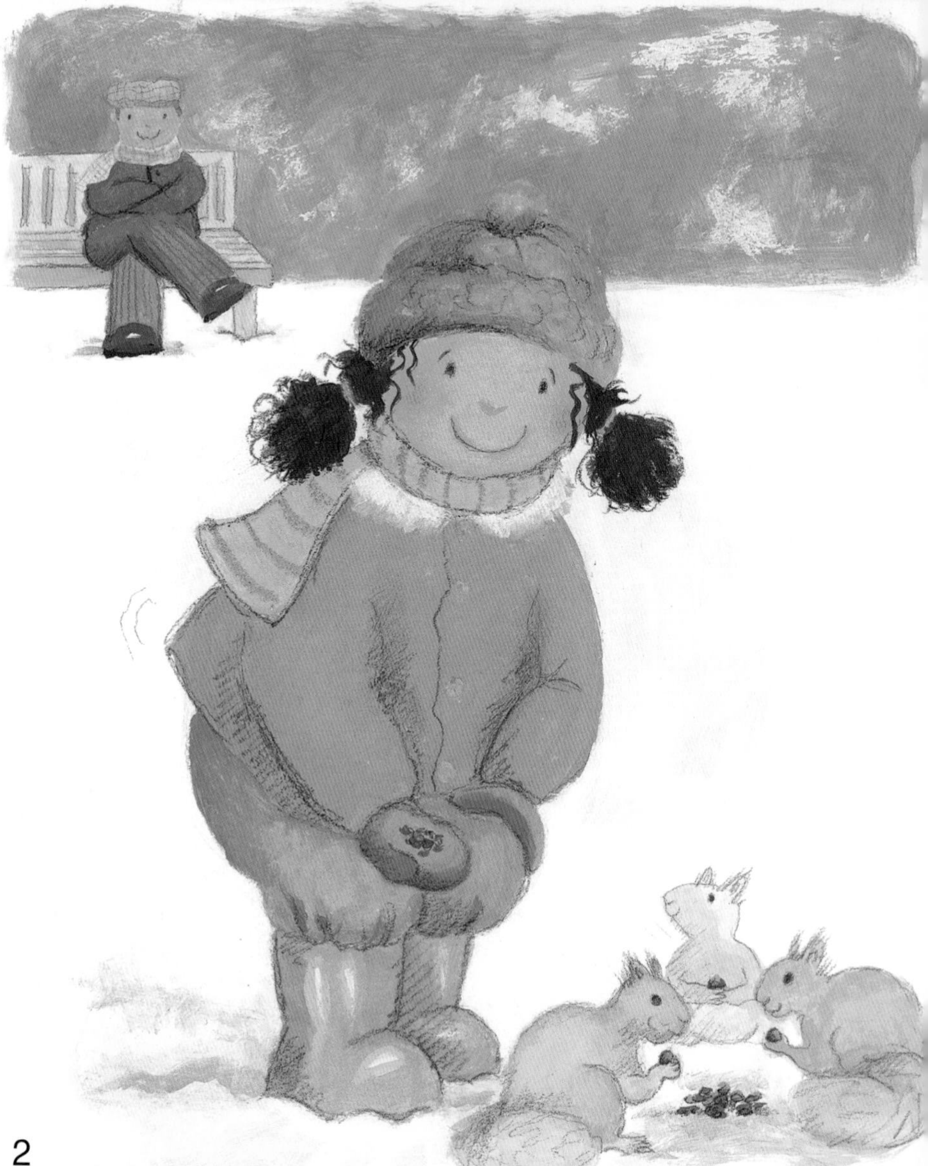

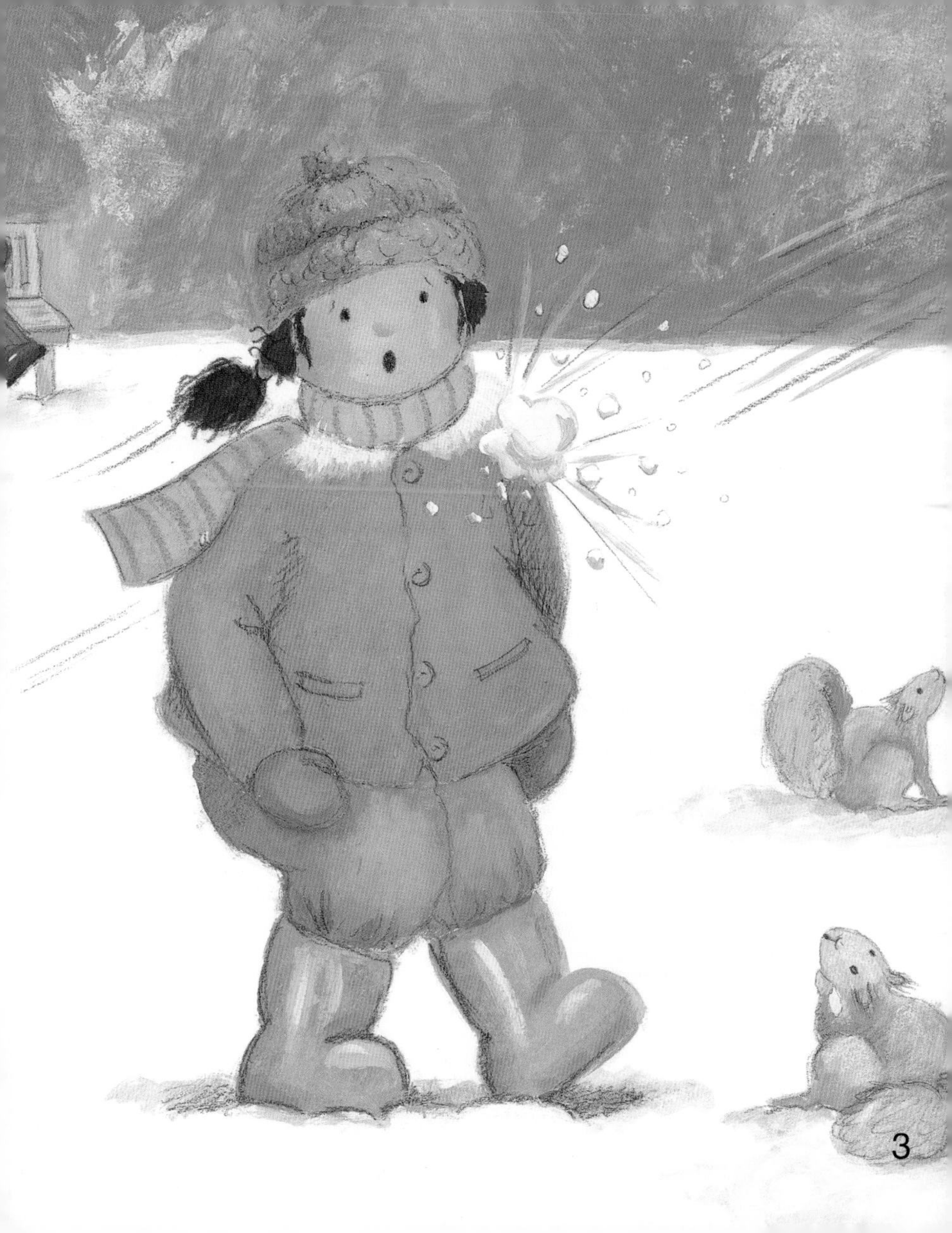

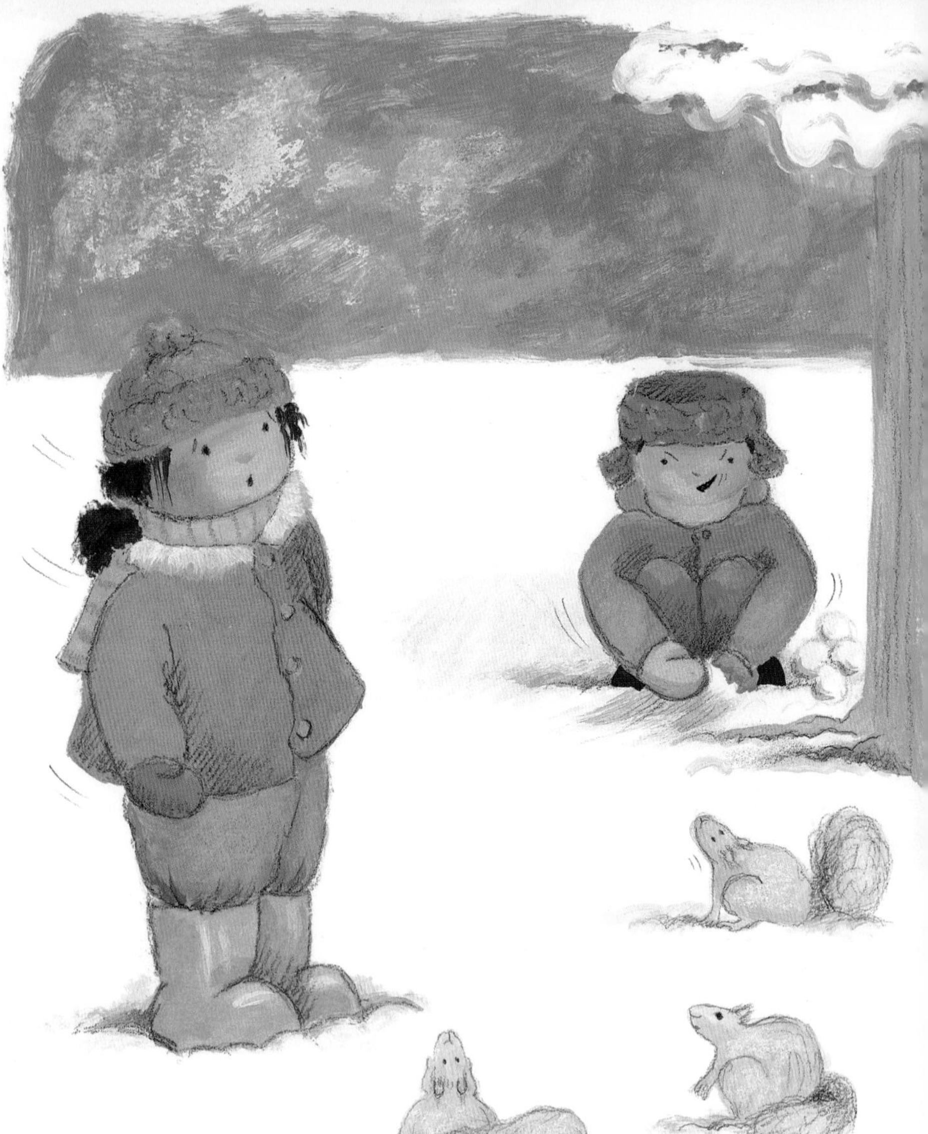

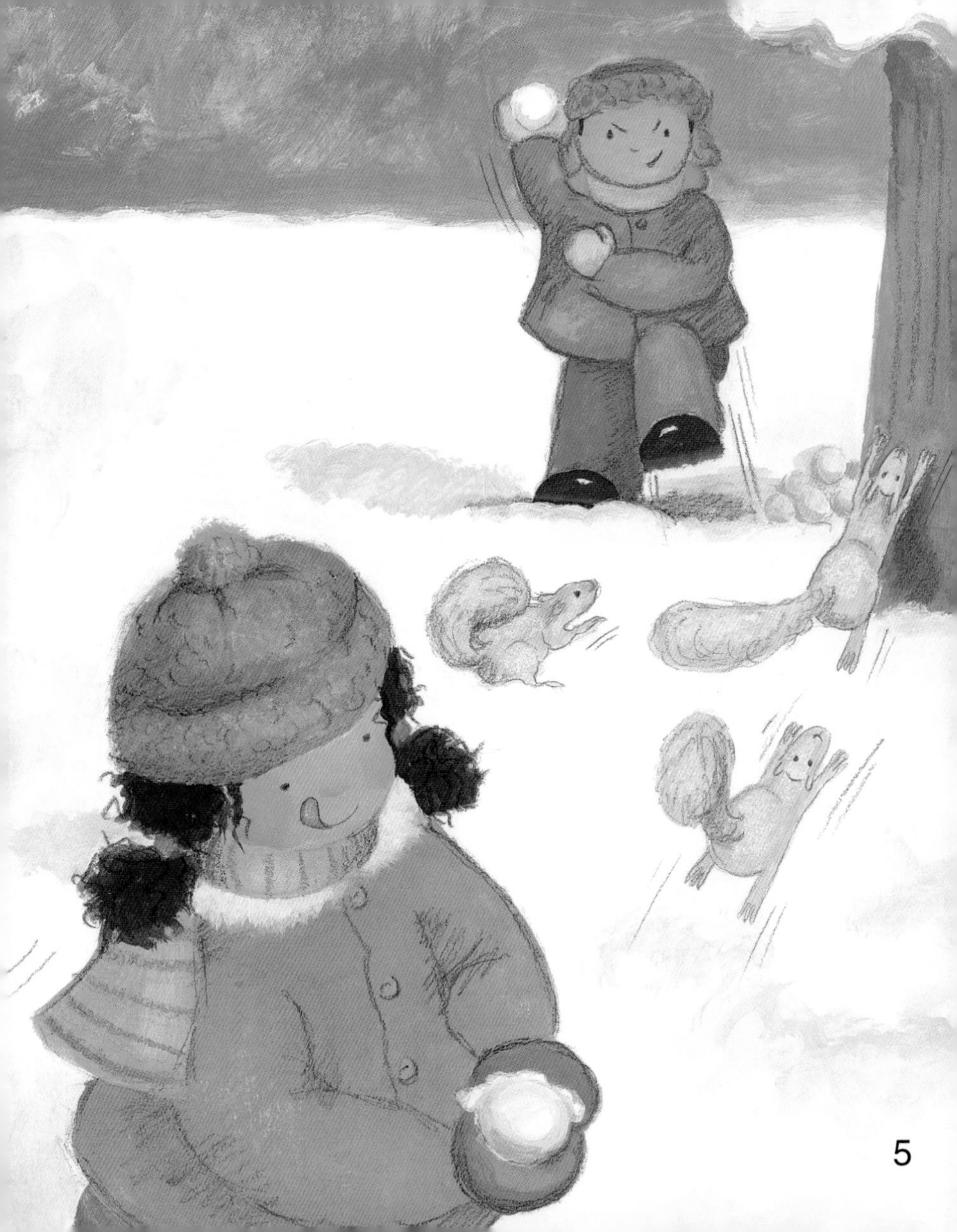

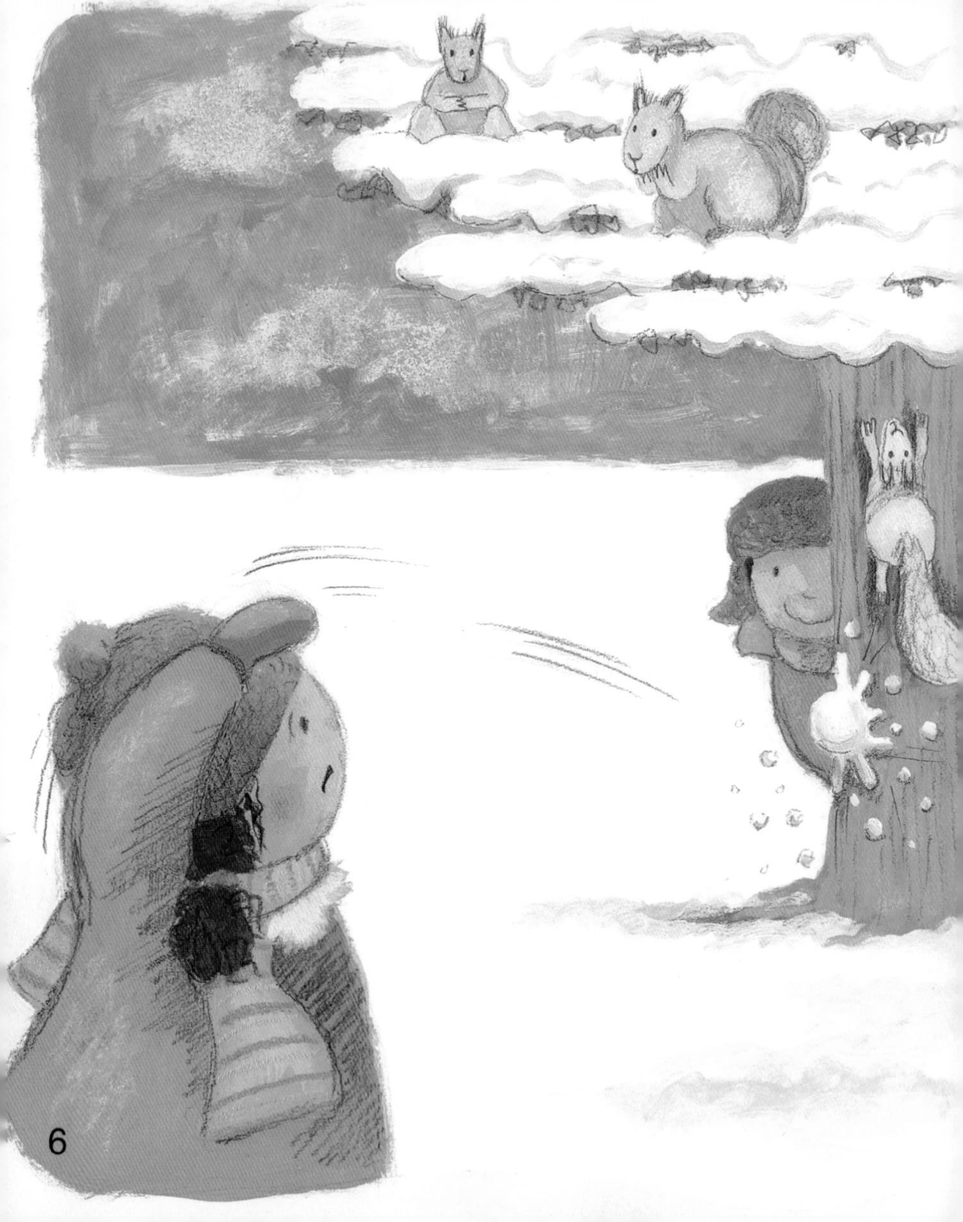

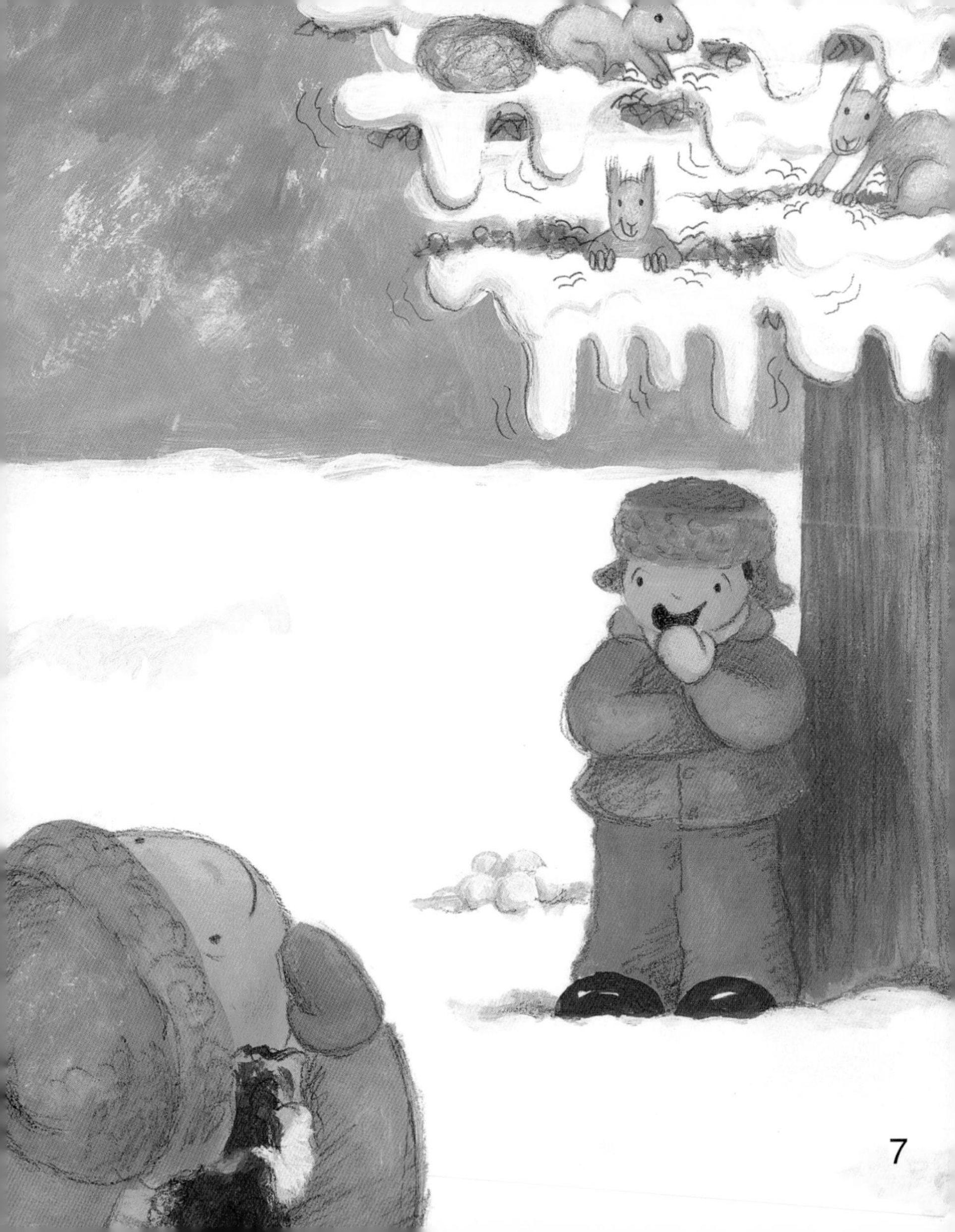

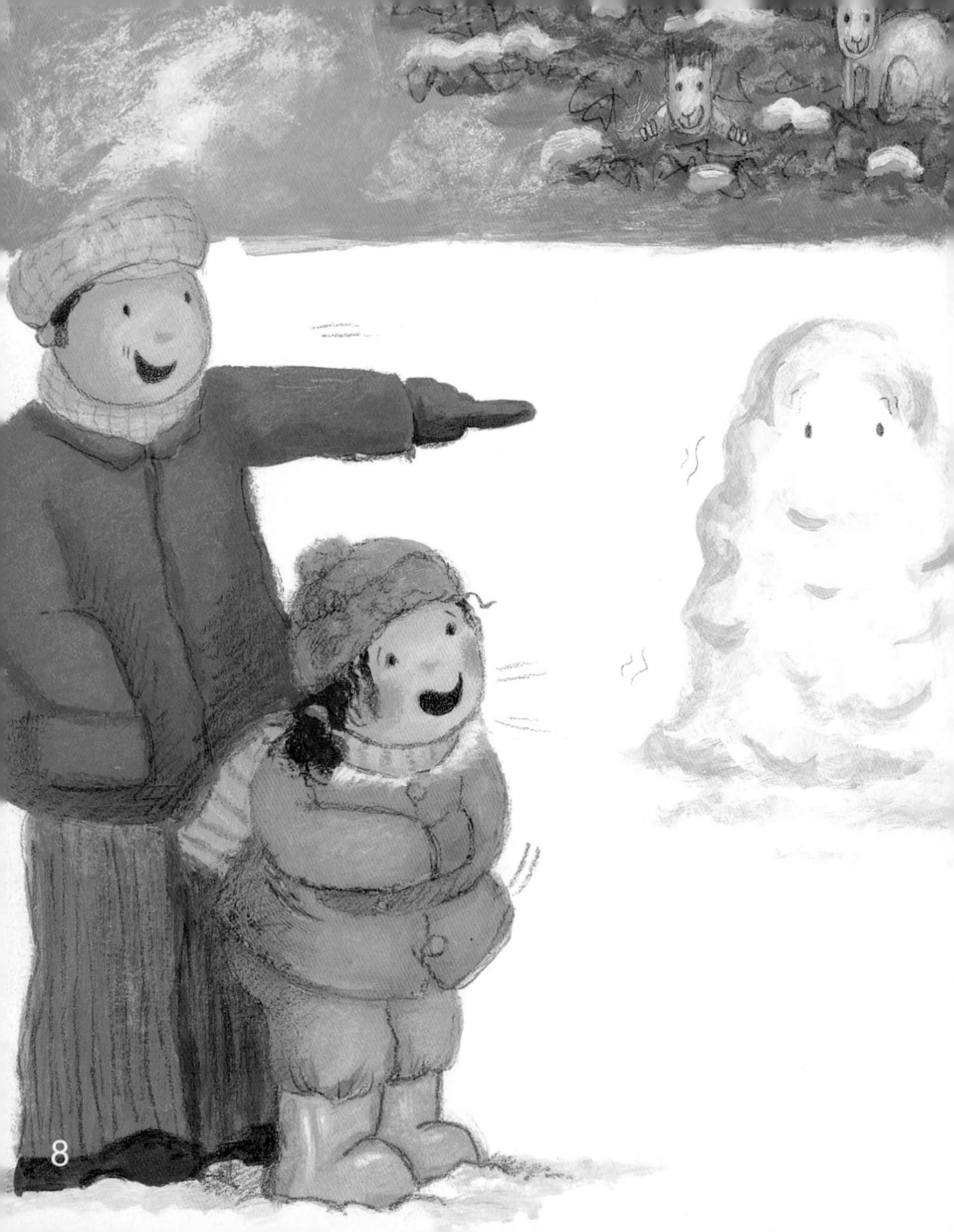